The Way You Run in Dreams

poems by

Tim Cremin

Finishing Line Press
Georgetown, Kentucky

The Way You Run in Dreams

Copyright © 2017 by Tim Cremin
ISBN 978-1-63534-333-5 First Edition
All rights reserved under International and Pan-American Copyright Conventions.
No part of this book may be reproduced in any manner whatsoever without written permission from the publisher, except in the case of brief quotations embodied in critical articles and reviews.

ACKNOWLEDGMENTS

"Three A.M. in the Kitchen," "Indian Ridge," and "At the Funeral Parlor" were included in the anthology, *Songs from the Castle's Remains*, Grey Court Poets.
"Cougar," "Totaled," and "Laboratory Notebook" were previously published by the *Eagle-Tribune*.
"Tweeting the Day Away" was previously published in *Crack the Spine*.
"His Trumpet" was previously published in *Schuylkill Valley Journal*.
"Mr. Beach" was previously published in *Forge*.
"At Marston's Landing" was previously published in *Albatross*.
"Just a Dance" was previously published in *WestWard Quarterly*.
"The No Man" was previously published in *Pennsylvania English*.
"Tomorrow the Moon" was previously published in *Westview*.
"Figures on a Beach," "Song About Heaven," and "Unplug the Night" were included in the anthology, *Merrimac Mic Anthology: Gleanings from the First Year*.
"Shortest Day at the Beach" was included in the anthology, *Shortest Day Longest Night*, Arachne Press.
"A Creature of the Air" was previously published in *Methuen Life*.
"I've Got Good News and Bad News" was previously published in *Poets Unlimited* on medium.com.

Publisher: Leah Maines
Editor: Christen Kincaid
Cover Art: From Wikimedia Commons, Lascaux replica, Common Domain
Author Photo: Pilar Quintana
Cover Design: Elizabeth Maines McCleavy

Printed in the USA on acid-free paper.
Order online: www.finishinglinepress.com
        also available on amazon.com

Author inquiries and mail orders:
Finishing Line Press
P. O. Box 1626
Georgetown, Kentucky 40324
U. S. A.

Table of Contents

Cougar 1
His Trumpet 2
Just a Dance 3
A Creature of the Air 4
At Marston's Landing 5
Pumpkin Carving Time 6
Three A.M. in the Kitchen 7
Parks Department Report 8
Song About Heaven 9
Shortest Day at the Beach 10
Tweeting the Day Away 11
Tomorrow the Moon 12
Unplug the Night 13
Indian Ridge 14
Valentine 15
Early March 16
At the Funeral Parlor 17
Planet Anura 18
The Ring Master 19
Mother's Day 20
The Way You Run in Dreams 21
I've Got Good News and Bad News 22
The No Man 23
Totaled 24
Figures on a Beach 25
Mr. Beach 26
Wildebeest Blues 27
Laboratory Notebook 28

For Pat, Liz, Sheila, and DJ

COUGAR

The cougar has been gone
from these mountains
a hundred-fifty years,
though I could swear
I've seen its tracks
a few times.

Maybe one raised in captivity
escaped or was released—
the initial thrill
of fully-stretched legs
gradually done in
by the need for skills
never learned when
capable of learning.

A twin-engine overhead
reminds me this isn't
true wilderness,
though the clouds, I would guess,
looked roughly the same
to my counterpart
a thousand years ago.

Could the cougar really come back?
Would its caterwaul rouse us
from our careless sleep?
Or have our ears gone deaf
to sound we used to hear
with every bone?

HIS TRUMPET

It didn't really hit me till I came
across his trumpet the day we cleared out the house.
I opened the case and saw it lying there,
silent from now on, though just the sight
of it was loud enough to sting my ears.

Up close, the brass was a funhouse mirror,
a Rube Goldberg of tubes and valves curving
around itself, somehow tuning the air
by the time it reached the end, the opening
where sound widens into unbounded space.

I had some interest in it as a kid,
and he tried to give me lessons for a while,
but then guitar and drums became everything—
my fragile self could not be seen with a horn,
though right at that moment, cold metal in

my hands, I wanted to make it ring again,
to kiss it, spit in it, and blow the walls down
with an elephant's triumphant blast.
So, pressing my lips to the mouthpiece,
I emptied my lungs in a decongestive fit.

"Now put a crease in it," I heard him say,
somehow speaking clearly from the grave.

JUST A DANCE

She takes your hand
and leads you to the middle
of the floor. It's just a dance—
don't read too much into it,

even though she holds on
an extra moment, after
the music stops.

A CREATURE OF THE AIR

The leaf was sure of being light enough
        to fly, if only it weren't tied to the tree.
And so a struggle ensued, lasting all summer;
        the slender stem could not break free.

Finally, the tree let go—
        the leaf was indeed a creature of the air
for a few gusting, tumbling, sailing seconds
        before the ground reclaimed what's hers.

AT MARSTON'S LANDING

The river god is trying to speak to you.
Not speak, exactly—maybe more like sing.
His rippled tongue is licking the sugary banks,
causing trees to lean, cling to what's left,
their last leaves whispering like a light rain.
Walking along, you cross a braided brook
giggling over rocks; crickets are holding
forth on the subject of Octobered earth.
On the other side, a new construction site
grinds out its daily quota of steel noise.
It's hard to hear as just another strain
of the god's fluid music—maybe more
like shards of the one glass silence shattering,
source of all sound, and all else flowing by.

PUMPKIN CARVING TIME

There aren't too many things
a twelve-year-old will do
with her father, so when she said OK
I had a rare coin in my pocket.

We cut out lids and started
scooping seeds for toasting
when the phone rang.

"Dad, can I go to the mall
with Caitlin and her Mom?"
Well, you can't compete with that
if all you've got are pumpkins,

even if it is the day
the trees let go of their leaves:
slow-motion fireworks,
volcanic billows of brilliant ash,
a flurry of peacock feathers,
swarms of brightly colored bats,
spray of divine fountains
called by the sun
to spring from the dirt.

THREE A.M. IN THE KITCHEN

God, the fridge is loud
when no other sound
stirs the room. Lately when sleep
gets interrupted, it's over.
Nothing more than usual—

another round of layoffs,
the mileage on the van,
the squeeze between
kids testing and failing parents.
How did Mom and Dad

stay above water,
paycheck to paycheck
for humpty-nine years?
Maybe the warm chaos of
"supper's almost ready"—

chicken under the broiler,
potatoes getting mashed,
steam condensing on the windows,
where I wrote my name
with my finger, over and over.

PARKS DEPARTMENT REPORT

The crumbling fountain,
overgrown with weeds,
still bubbles in the middle,
though now at a less-than-majestic
height. Coins are rare

and disappear; the pigeons
have moved on.
Not the scorpion—
still poised within the broken

stone—a blade of fire
staving off the ice.
Done molting, but hunger

persists. May it never
end.

SONG ABOUT HEAVEN

In case you didn't
recognize the lyrics
recited by the doctor
on the seventh floor,

the elevator opens to
the spacious lobby
being filled by a harpist
with the tune.

SHORTEST DAY AT THE BEACH

No gulls, just one crow
to start the Darkness Festival.
Poor thing—one bleak note
like a rock caught in its throat.

I guess that's as high as the sun
is going to get. We must be
further north than I thought.

TWEETING THE DAY AWAY

Gone in search of a vision.
First in line at the traffic lights.
Listening in at the weird end of the dial.
Dissolving myself in song.
Filling in more of my map.
Dulling the point of my pencil.
Picking at that scab again.
Tripping over my clumsy tongue.
Falling a little further behind.
Coming up for air.
Embracing the noise.
Fraying my cuffs.
In an icebreaker cutting through the frozen sound.
Trying to hit four targets with one shot.
Letting the game teach me how to play.
Setting an elaborate trap for myself.
Ignoring warning signs.
Chasing the pain around my body.
Watching stars fall to earth.
Having trouble connecting the dots.
Outliving my way of life.
Getting one more squeeze from the toothpaste tube.
Dreaming.
Still dreaming.

TOMORROW THE MOON

Tonight we'll rest;
tomorrow the moon
will be close to full—
maybe there'll be
enough light on the trail
to walk the woods,
where history is written
in concentric rings;
maybe we'll hear
stars speak
their wordless language,
bringing all the past
into each night's sky.

Tonight we'll rest;
we'll bank our fires
while watery dreams
engulf us in timelessness.
Maybe tomorrow
we'll stay up late
to wonder about time.
Does it pass
like hourglass sand
from future to past
through now's thin neck?
Does it accumulate
like data
encoded in our cells?
Is each moment eternal—
still traveling like starlight
across the universe?
Tonight we'll rest.

UNPLUG THE NIGHT

On a midnight descent you see
the luminous beast sprawled out below,
bright scales spiraling wildly around
its head, tentacles extending
in every direction to capture
more of the dreaming ground.

Unplug the night! Clear the foggy dome
of our electric waste. Let starlight fall
unfiltered on our eyes, restore our vision
of skies so drenched with stars
they river through the dark
like a cataract of light.

INDIAN RIDGE

When I first saw
this thirty-foot wave
of glacial silt snaking
through the woods like
an upside-down river,
I could hardly imagine
mile-thick ice, flowing
under its own weight,
bulldozing through here
ten-thousand years ago,
its meltwater leaving
this ready-made path
for the people who
first chased the herds
into the warming valley
of Merrimack, the
place of strong current
that sustained their hunt
for hundreds of generations.
Now the tom tom of walking here
takes me back to them,
back to that ice age
and the ones before,
back till I can almost recall
what it is that seems forgotten,
back where I can start over—
and this time maybe
not lose my way.

VALENTINE

A blast of wind shreds the last
of the office agenda as I cross
the parking lot. Venus—like a coin flip
caught by a camera's flash—

delivers some light but no heat;
I worm through the dark toward warmth.
Spooned in our bed, doubly warm,

we have no need of light. Venus (unseen)
is close by, and seems a true goddess,

deserving of prayer if not worship.

EARLY MARCH

The dog and I on an early morning walk:
the trail pulls us—the way words on a page
pull eyes—to water pouring over rock,
cascading prayers murmured for every age.
We catch our breath and watch the stream exhale;
blood flow swamps the sting of winter air.
The dog looks up and wags her eager tail—
she knows my schedule has no time to spare.
But something keeps me for a look around:
change in the air, a sense that what's ahead
has already started stirring in the ground.
I ought to go; decide to stay instead.
The schedule can go on without me today,
so I can watch winter washing away.

AT THE FUNERAL PARLOR

Giant granite steps and her bare hand
stinging cold from the black iron railing,
the room too full of flowers and grown-ups,
Bubba in the casket, deaf to all
the solemn murmurs, looking like himself
except for the sealed lips (purple and dry)
and rosary-cuffed hands. Hard to believe
that night was nearly eighty years ago.

This time it's her last first cousin (Lord knows
how many in between). Will anyone
be left to see her waked? She's even outlived
her undertaker—his son will have to lay her out.
Now there's talk of closing down the parish—
just her luck: one sacrament left. At least
the plot's all set, the stone already there—
just need to chisel in the final year.

PLANET ANURA

Moonlight shadows me along the road
to April's marsh, where alien sleigh bells
ring out of the mud, pulling me in
till I'm immersed in sound, till I'm

an alien on their damp planet.
I wish I could save
this fountain of sonic flares

so we could share it later.
I miss it already, even though

I'm here in the middle of it happening.

THE RING MASTER

Inside my tent, where gravity is defied,
Your spirit will rise, your sluggish heart will race—
Come join the magic happening inside.

With your own eyes, see jugglers' clubs that glide
Like spinning spokes, filling their circled space
Inside my tent, where gravity is defied.

Majestic horses take their turns in stride;
The air is charged as sight and sound embrace—
Come join the magic happening inside.

See acrobats perform what's never been tried,
And make it look easy, with style and grace,
Inside my tent, where gravity is defied.

Did you ever laugh so hard you almost cried?
My clowns can put a smile on any face—
Come join the magic happening inside.

Step right up, folks—let me be your guide.
We'll rise above this ordinary place,
Inside my tent, where gravity is defied—
Come join the magic happening inside.

MOTHER'S DAY

The last load is in the dryer,
so she'll pour herself a beer
and give Helen a call
to unwind.

More cracks have appeared,
so she'll pour a little more
of her heart out to seal them,

pull a little harder
to keep us in her orbit,

lest we veer off into the dark.

THE WAY YOU RUN IN DREAMS

The Preakness is my favorite—we find out
if the Derby winner gets a shot
at the Triple Crown. The best one I ever saw
was back in eighty-nine, when Easy Goer
was favored to bounce back after Sunday Silence
won the Derby on a muddy track.

Well, down the lane they came, neck and neck,
chestnut and black—a photo finish—the black
one by a nose. The caption might have read,
"Sunday Silence: legend in the making;
Easy Goer: promise unfulfilled."

He went off an underdog at Belmont,
and seemed to be, like his sire, Alydar,
destined to prove his rival's supremacy.
All at once he surged ahead, broke free—
began to run the way you run in dreams:
those long, flowing, low-gravity strides;
horse and jockey locked together,
charging toward perfection.

I'VE GOT GOOD NEWS AND BAD NEWS

The bad news is the bridge
you're crossing is burning down
behind you, collapsing
underneath each step you take.

The good news is
you only need to use it
once.

THE NO MAN

Dad's in the den with a highball
and Nancy Sinatra, trying to unstoop
after another day's indignities—
stuff he'll never tell me about

that nonetheless is sinking in,
along with this growing likeness
I tried to swear off, this being
a bystander to one's own life.

After he died I waited for weeks
to unlock the bottom drawer
of his desk, afraid of finding
the nothing that was there.

TOTALED

"Totaled," was all he said, eyes on the wreck
as he circled it, change as always
jingling in his pocket. And he would know,
having worked his way up from claim adjuster
to whatever he is now. He wouldn't say more—
would rather I taunt myself with what he must
be thinking, having given me the car
a month ago—not a scratch in its six years,
and every scheduled maintenance done. And me
not knowing squat about insurance or cars,
and not caring to listen even if
he tried to tell me how long he saved up
his paper route money to buy his first car
because nobody ever gave him anything
he had to earn it all, so now do I feel
close enough to worthless?

FIGURES ON A BEACH

The child gives chase
to catch a fallen
crescent moonlet
or scatter them all
back to the sky,

screaming glee
at flashing wings
in frantic lift,
speechless gaze
at stringless kites.

Again, again—
chaste desire
flooding the sand;
no sign of tiring.
The older kids
don't bother trying.

MR. BEACH

"Excuse me, sir. Could you watch our boards
while we go out on the jetty to dive off the tower?"

"Sure." Why not? I'm just sitting here
with my book, lacquered in SPF 30.

"Go feet first—it's not high tide yet."
Listen to me, as if I went feet first

when thick-haired, in cut-off jeans,
and claiming no dependents.

Look at the two of them:
cocksure as rock stars;

head first, of course,
right back up for more;

dripping with sunlight,
just fitting into their skin.

They remind me of me
before I felt my limits,

when I thought there might
not be any.

WILDEBEEST BLUES

We'd better hurry up and join the stampede
so we don't get left behind.

                                        Never mind.
Let them go, charging ahead as if
they're on some kind of mission, and not just stuck
in the middle of the herd, trying to keep up.

Even if you made it to the front,
what would that get you? First one over
the cliff? Let's stay here, take a look
around, enjoy the long grass for a while.

I know the lions will come in silence
and can't be outrun or thrown off the scent.
I'd rather their teeth find my softest flesh
than be trampled by my own kind.

LABORATORY NOTEBOOK

September   The rotting sweetness
of soft apples on the ground
beside Tucker Road.

October   Yesterday's storm knocked
some color out of the trees,
but our feet don't mind.

November   Didn't see much more
than two tails bounding away
to mesh with the woods.

December   This time every year
the pond grows a skin of ice,
but still we're surprised.

January   Good night for a walk:
high moon, clear sky, bare trees, and
light snow on the trail.

February   Our spirits soaring
above our bodies walking
on Five Crossings Trail.

March   Some of last night's snow
still clings to the grey branches,
revealing more truth.

April   Here life and death are
tangled so tightly, it's hard
to tell them apart.

May   The great oaks stretch out
their green nets to catch the sun,
turn it into tree.

June   Ruthless mosquitoes
        forgive not those who trespass
        without repellent.

July   Squinting to look at
        the clover field's purple dress
        shimmering with sun.

August On top of Holt Hill
        the cricket clock is counting
        down the days till fall.

Tim Cremin was born and raised in Lowell, Massachusetts as the fifth of Kay and Dan Cremin's eight children. He earned a degree in Chemical Engineering from the University of Massachusetts Lowell, and worked several years as a mathematics teacher while earning an MS in Mathematics from Salem State University. He changed careers and started working as an actuary as he and his wife, Pat, made plans for bringing children into their life.

After completing the actuarial professional exams, Tim rekindled his interest in writing poetry. His poetry was first published in the *Eagle-Tribune* newspaper's Annual Spring Poetry Contest, including a first-place award in 2005 for the poem, "Cougar." He has been a member of the Grey Court Poets (a community poetry group based in Methuen, Massachusetts) for several years, and has posted many Grey Court members' video performances on their YouTube channel (https://youtube.com/user/GreyCourtPoets). The YouTube channel also features video slide shows Tim created for collaborative projects of the Grey Court Poets and the Arts Institute Group of the Merrimack Valley.

Tim has performed featured readings sponsored by the Robert Frost Foundation and other local poetry groups and organizations. His poetry has been published in *Forge, Pennsylvania English, Poetry Pacific, Schuylkill Valley Journal, Westview,* and other publications. Tim's work can also be found online at https://medium.com/@tim.cremin. He lives in Andover, Massachusetts with his wife Pat, daughters Liz and Sheila, son DJ, grandson Kieran, and mother-in-law Alma.

www.ingramcontent.com/pod-product-compliance
Lightning Source LLC
LaVergne TN
LVHW041509070426
835507LV00012B/1446